ALPHABET ANTICS

Hundreds of Activities to Challenge and Enrich Letter Learners of All Ages

Illustrated and Written
by

Ken Vinton

Edited by Pamela Espeland

free Spirit
PUBLISHING

Library of Congress Cataloging-in-Publication Data

Vinton, Ken.
    Alphabet antics: hundreds of activities to challenge and enrich letter learners of all ages /
by Ken Vinton.
      p.   cm.
   ISBN: 1–57542–008–2
  1. Alphabet—History—Study and teaching.   2. Alphabets—Study and teaching.   I. Title.
P211.V48   1996
428.1—dc20

               96–15616
               CIP

Design and production by MacLean & Tuminelly

10 9 8 7 6 5 4 3 2 1

Printed in the United States of America

Free Spirit Publishing Inc.
400 First Avenue North, Suite 616
Minneapolis, MN 55401-1730
(612) 338-2068
help4kids@freespirit.com

DEDICATION

This book is dedicated to the growing group that surrounds me with love, laughter, learning, and life . . . my family. *Left to right:* Mary Ann, Ali, Ryan (holding Majic), Me (holding Inxs), and BUG N OUT.

CONTENTS · CONTENTS · CONTENTS

INTRODUCTION

1

A BRIEF CARTOON
LOOK AT
OUR LETTER
HISTORY

3

ALPHABET ANTICS A TO Z

7

CONTENTS · CONTENTS · CONTENTS

MORE ALPHABETS

113

ALPHABET BORDERS

125

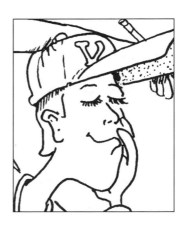

ABOUT THE AUTHOR

135

INTRODUCTION

I've been interested in the alphabet, primarily individual letters and their aesthetic appeal to an artist, for a long time. The more I investigated the 26 letters we use every day, the more fun I had with the information I found.

It's intriguing to discover where the alphabet came from. Ancient cultures had myths and stories to explain the origins of their letters. The Greeks thought that Cadmus, a great hero, brought 16 letters from Phoenicia. This belief was based in truth, because the Greeks did borrow many of the Phoenician forms—which the Phoenicians had borrowed from the Egyptians. The Egyptians believed that the god Thoth, who looked like a man with the head of an ibis, invented the hieroglyphics—their alphabet. The Chinese believed that a dragon-looking four-eyed man named Ts'ang Chien founded their characters.

Approximately 200 alphabets have come and gone that we know about. (Think about the hundreds we've missed because of lack of information, no records, small regions, etc.) Today about 50 alphabets flourish worldwide. The English alphabet is the most popular; with it (and slight variations), people write in English, French, Spanish, Portuguese, Italian, Dutch, German, Polish, Norwegian, Swedish, and Danish.

We take our alphabet for granted. Many people think that it's just "always been there." I wondered where each character came from originally. How did each one change over 600,000 years? Why do we angle each letter a certain way? I touch on these questions and more in *Alphabet Antics*.

How to Use This Book

I can't tell you exactly how to use this book because there is no "right" way to use it. Instead, I'll explain what's in it and offer suggestions for you to try. It's my hope that these suggestions will kickstart your creative thinking—that you'll come up with your own ideas for projects and enrichment activities based on the information included here.

A Brief Cartoon Look at Our Letter History (pages 3–6) is an illustrated "short story" of how our alphabet came to be. Letter learners who want to know more might research the history of writing, papyrus, books, paper—and the meaning of "triskaidekaphobic."

Alphabet Antics A to Z (pages 7–111) is the main body of the book. Here you'll find 26 four-page mini-chapters, one for each letter of the alphabet. Each mini-chapter includes two reproducible illustrated pages and two pages of text.

The illustrated pages are:

- a "negative space" drawing of the letter (the letter itself isn't drawn, but outlined by the illustrations that surround it). I thought these might make great alphabet borders to color and post around the room—but that's just one idea.
- a "border page" featuring things, critters, etc. that start with the letter. These pages can be used in many ways—for creative writing (stories, poems, plays, scenes, essays, etc.), journaling, reports, paragraphs, letters, outlines, and also, of course, for drawing and doodling.

On the text pages, you'll find:

- a quotation by someone whose name begins with the letter. You might find these useful for journaling or discussions.
- "Fun Facts" about the letter—interesting trivia tidbits to share.
- a "Project" suggestion that starts with the letter. These are writing, drawing, and thinking activities I have tried with my own students and found to be successful. (You'll notice that I subscribe to the school of thinking skills.)
- three "Find Out About . . ." lists of people, places, and "potpourri" (a grab-bag of possibilities). All 24 items are potential topics for papers, projects, plays, presentations, and more.
- lists of "Words" and "Challenge Words" for mini-spelling tests, writing exercises, look-it-up projects, or whatever else you choose.
- a "History" section that briefly traces the origins of each letter both verbally and visually.
- a "What's in the Picture?" list that identifies the things and critters on the border page. Don't be surprised if your students or children see things that aren't listed here. A starred word (or words) points out the emotion or affect I have tried to portray with one of the critters; again, please don't let my interpretation serve as the final word.
- an " . . . In More Alphabets" section that shows the various forms the letter takes in the Manual, Semaphore, Braille, International Flag Code, Morse Code, and NATO Code alphabets. As you know, kids love codes.

More Alphabets (pages 113–124) includes full-page illustrated versions of the Manual, Semaphore, Braille, etc., alphabets to share, plus a few additions.

Finally, **Alphabet Borders** (pages 125–133) is a bonus section of eight illustrated border pages, each featuring the complete English alphabet.

My philosophy on writing a book is the same general approach I take to everything I do: Have fun and the results will turn out okay. I hope you have as much fun using *Alphabet Antics* as I had putting it together. I would love to hear your thoughts, ideas, and impressions. Please write to me c/o Free Spirit Publishing Inc., 400 First Avenue North, Suite 616, Minneapolis, MN 55401-1730.

Enjoy!

Ken Vinton
Indiana, Pennsylvania

NEW **OLD**

A BRIEF CARTOON LOOK AT OUR LETTER HISTORY

COME ON, FOLLOW ALONG!

...AS TOLD BY THE TOOLS THAT CREATED THE ALPHABET YOU KNOW TODAY.

At first the letters were not written but chiseled in marble or pressed into wax. This made the letters look stiff or different from the look of letters today. The Phoenicians took ideas from the Egyptians and made a simplified group of letters that the Greeks modified and then the Romans smoothed out to create the so-called "modern" alphabet.

OUCH!

Many adaptations of each letter occurred along the way. The ancients first read up and down, then backwards (right to left). To confuse things more, next they read from right to left, then dropped down one line and read from left to right. This was known as the ox-turn (boustrophedon). Complicated?

Whew! In time, the ancients got tired of the confusion, and simplicity came to the rescue.

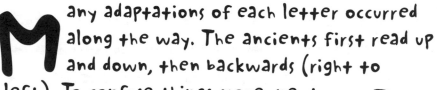

STINK

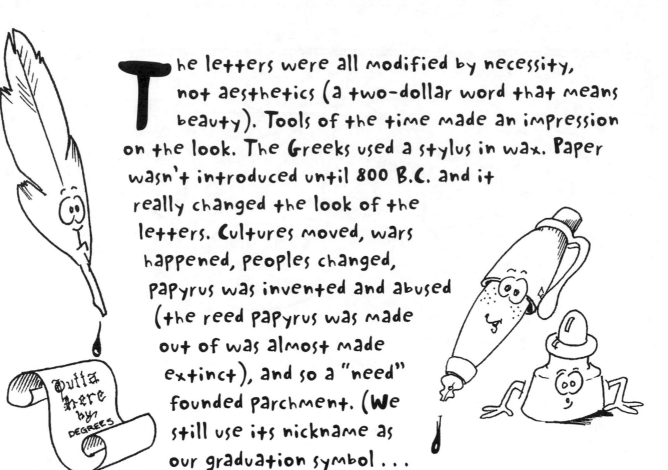

The letters were all modified by necessity, not aesthetics (a two-dollar word that means beauty). Tools of the time made an impression on the look. The Greeks used a stylus in wax. Paper wasn't introduced until 800 B.C. and it really changed the look of the letters. Cultures moved, wars happened, peoples changed, papyrus was invented and abused (the reed papyrus was made out of was almost made extinct), and so a "need" founded parchment. (We still use its nickname as our graduation symbol . . . the "sheepskin.")

Outta here by DEGREES

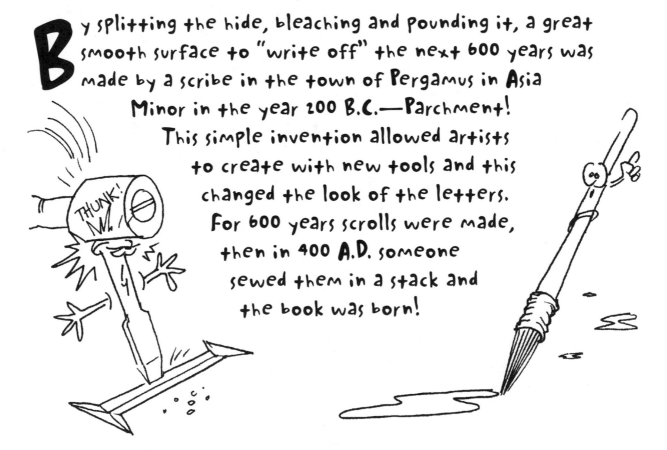

By splitting the hide, bleaching and pounding it, a great smooth surface to "write off" the next 600 years was made by a scribe in the town of Pergamus in Asia Minor in the year 200 B.C.—Parchment! This simple invention allowed artists to create with new tools and this changed the look of the letters. For 600 years scrolls were made, then in 400 A.D. someone sewed them in a stack and the book was born!

THUNK!

The Greeks gave us the word for our group of letters—"Alphabet"— from their first two letters, Alpha and Beta.

Everyone wanted books, and many scribes tired of endless hours of scribing. They took shortcuts. After many years the "tongues" needed more sounds, so they made new letters for these new sounds.

One example of change is the letter D. It started out life as the Egyptian hieroglyph ▤ that meant "door." It was simplified to ⊔. In Hieratic script it was ⌂. The Phoenicians wrote it as ⌂. The Greeks modified it to Δ, and the Romans tipped it over and rounded it off to make our D.

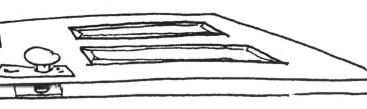

Thirteen of the Greek letters were taken over exactly as they were by the Romans. When the Romans needed ten more sounds, they developed by change the C, F, G, L, P, Q, R, S, V, and D.

The Z was not needed by the Romans, so the 6th letter of the Greek alphabet (Zeta) was kicked out. But later (tick-tick-tick) they realized they needed this Zound! They put it back but in a new order—last! The poor letters J, U, W waited 1000 or more years to be invented and used.

The march of History takes us on mysterious paths. Where will our letters evolve next???

A a

"We all live under the same sky, but we don't have the same horizon."

Konrad Adenauer

FUN FACTS

The saying "A-OK" ("perfect, excellent, fine") was introduced by Project Mercury astronauts during Commander Alan B. Shephard's flight on May 5, 1961. "A-Number-1" ("first class, excellent") comes from a system once used to classify ships; the Class A, Number 1 ship was the newest and fastest. People who have a "Type A" personality are impatient, competitive, and aggressive.

PROJECT

Anthropomorphize. To "anthropomorphize" means to give human characteristics to something that isn't human. Think about, write about, or draw an object or animal. Then give it human characteristics.

FIND OUT ABOUT...

People	Places	Potpourri
Hank Aaron	Afghanistan	Abominable Snowman
Louisa May Alcott	Amazon River	ACLU
Alexander the Great	Amsterdam	Air Pollution
Hans Christian Andersen	Antarctica	Alligators
Maya Angelou	Appalachia	Angels
Johnny Appleseed	Argentina	April Fools' Day
Louis Armstrong	Atlanta	Archaeology
King Arthur	Australia	Asteroids

WORDS

ace	age	ant
acorn	air	arch
admit	alert	atom

CHALLENGE WORDS

abominable	ambidextrous	aqueduct
accentuate	anthology	assuage
affable	anthropomorphism	azure

HISTORY

The letter A comes from the Phoenician "Aleph," which meant "ox." The Greeks took Aleph, turned it on its side, and called it "Alpha." The Romans made it look the way it does today.

PHOENICIAN	OLD HEBREW	EARLY GREEK	CLASSICAL GREEK

ETRUSCAN	EARLY LATIN	MODERN ROMAN

WHAT'S IN THE PICTURE?

Clockwise from top

Arched Aqueduct

Addition (2 + 2)

Ant

Airplane

Anteater

Amazed, Astonished★

Abstract Art

Ace

"A" IN MORE ALPHABETS

MANUAL ALPHABET

SEMAPHORE

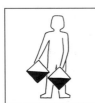

BRAILLE

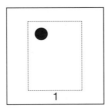

1

INTERNATIONAL FLAG CODE

MORSE CODE

NATO CODE

Alpha (AL-FAH)

B b

"Be curious always! For knowledge will not acquire you; you must acquire it."

Sudie Back

FUN FACTS

B is a musical note and the chemical symbol for Boron. When joined with another B, it's a tiny copper shot for a Red Ryder BB gun. And it sounds like any of several winged, often stinging insects that gather pollen and nectar from flowers . . . a Bee.

PROJECT

Brainstorm backwards. Either draw or write with your opposite hand for one day (or one hour or one period—whatever time frame you choose). Experience the remarkable "crossover" effects of the brain. *Or:* Try writing script in reverse (backwards). Then look up "Leonardo da Vinci" and find out about his secret note-taking skills.

FIND OUT ABOUT...

People	Places	Potpourri
P.T. Barnum	Babylon	Bacteria
The Beatles	Baltimore	Baseball
Alexander Graham Bell	Bangkok	Berlin Wall
Yogi Berra	Bangladesh	Big Bang Theory
Judy Blume	Beirut	Boston Tea Party
Simón Bolívar	Big Horn	Brainwashing
Daniel Boone	Bosnia	Butterflies
Gwendolyn Brooks	Bulgaria	Byte

WORDS

bag	best	boat
bang	bike	box
barn	blank	bye-bye

CHALLENGE WORDS

bacteria	basal	bittersweet
ballistics	bibliophile	brainchild
baroque	binary	bureaucracy

HISTORY

The letter B started out as the Phoenician "Beth," which meant "house." The Greeks borrowed Beth, flipped it, and turned it into "Beta." The Romans rounded out the shape that we still use today.

PHOENICIAN	OLD HEBREW	EARLY GREEK	CLASSICAL GREEK
9	9	δ	B

EARLY LATIN	MODERN ROMAN
B	Bb

WHAT'S IN THE PICTURE?

Clockwise from top

Banner

Broom

Bugle

Boxing Betta fish

Bee

Belligerent★

Bell

Bird

"B" IN MORE ALPHABETS

MANUAL ALPHABET

SEMAPHORE

BRAILLE

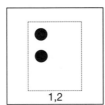

1,2

INTERNATIONAL FLAG CODE

MORSE CODE

NATO CODE

Bravo
(BRAH-VOH)

14

FUN FACTS

The C clef is a sign in musical notation that indicates which line of a musical staff represents middle C. In slang, to "hit a high C" means to shriek loudly. C is also the chemical symbol for Carbon. In Roman numerals, C stands for 100, which is why some people call a $100 bill a "C-note."

PROJECT

Create. What would you like to create today? A song? A dance? A poem? A picture? A model? A dozen cookies? A dream? Be *creative* as you *celebrate* and *commemorate* the letter C.

FIND OUT ABOUT...

People	Places	Potpourri
Calamity Jane	Calcutta	Capillaries
Jimmy Carter	Camelot	Carbon dating
George Washington Carver	Cape of Good Hope	CAT scan
Mary Cassatt	Caracas	Censorship
Cesar Chavez	Chicago	CIA
Winston Churchill	Chile	Clichés
Ty Cobb	Copenhagen	Crickets
Crazy Horse	Czechoslovakia	Cupid

WORDS

cage	center	cold
call	charge	cool
cartoon	click	cube

CHALLENGE WORDS

cajole	capacious	clique
calculate	Cenozoic	confidential
cantilever	cerulean	crevasse

"Life is the art of drawing without an eraser."

John Christians

HISTORY

The letter C began as the Phoenician "Gimel," which meant "camel." The Greeks turned it into "Gamma"—their G. The Romans rounded it into a C, and at first they used that symbol for both the G sound and the K sound. Later they put a bar on the C and created the G we know today.

PHOENICIAN	OLD HEBREW	EARLY GREEK	CLASSICAL GREEK
𐤂	𐤂	Λ	Γ

ETRUSCAN	EARLY LATIN	MODERN ROMAN
>	<	Cc

WHAT'S IN THE PICTURE?

Clockwise from top

Crescent moon

Cosmonaut Cow

Chicken

Chair

Cup of Coffee

Cat

Cello

Choking, Coughing*

Compass

Crown

Cube

"C" IN MORE ALPHABETS

MANUAL ALPHABET

SEMAPHORE

BRAILLE

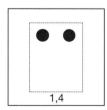

1,4

INTERNATIONAL FLAG CODE

MORSE CODE

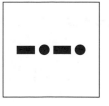

NATO CODE

Charlie
(CHAR-LEE)

D d

FUN FACTS

"D-Day" was the code name given to the invasion of Nazi-occupied France on June 6, 1944. The victory of the Allies in Europe began on this day. D is also the chemical symbol for Deuterium. In Roman numerals, D means 500. In sports, D stands for "defense."

PROJECT

Dramatize something. Make slips of paper that describe various processes, movements, etc. and place them in a hat. Pull one randomly and, without speaking, act it out. *Example:* You're a piece of bacon in a frying pan with the heat gradually increasing . . . .

FIND OUT ABOUT...

People	Places	Potpourri
Dalai Lama	Damascus	Dark Ages
Salvador Dali	Danube River	Déjà vu
Deng Xiaoping	Dead Sea	Dipper (Big or Little)
Emily Dickinson	Death Valley	DNA
Dionne Quintuplets	Denmark	Dogs
Walt Disney	District of Columbia	Doppler effect
Dracula	Dominican Republic	Dragonflies
W.E.B. Du Bois	Dublin	Dreams

WORDS

dance	dig	dive
day	dime	draw
deep	dish	duck

CHALLENGE WORDS

Dakota	demarcation	diphthong
debris	deoxyribonucleic acid	dromedary
debutante	diorama	dyslexia

HISTORY

The letter D comes from the Phoenician "Daleth," which meant "door" because it looked like a tent flap. The Greeks took Daleth and named it "Delta." Later the letter was turned on its side and rounded. The Romans borrowed Delta and made it look the way it does today.

PHOENICIAN	OLD HEBREW	EARLY GREEK	CLASSICAL GREEK

EARLY LATIN	MODERN ROMAN

WHAT'S IN THE PICTURE?

Clockwise from top

Dirigible

Door with Doorknob

Donut

Dachshund

Detonator

Dizzy★

Dumbbell

Doll with Diamond

Duck

"D" IN MORE ALPHABETS

MANUAL ALPHABET

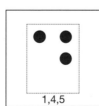

SEMAPHORE

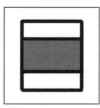

BRAILLE

1,4,5

INTERNATIONAL FLAG CODE

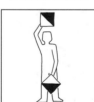

MORSE CODE

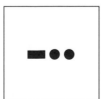

NATO CODE

Delta
(DELL-TAH)

E e

"Adventure is worthwhile in itself."

Amelia Earhart

FUN FACTS

E is the most frequently used letter of the English alphabet. In Einstein's famous equation, $E = mc^2$, it stands for "energy." If you've ever sent or received E-mail, you know that it also stands for "electronic." "E.T." is the abbreviation most people use for "extraterrestrial"—something (or someone) from another world.

PROJECT

Enlighten a black-and-white photocopy of a famous work of art. Re-create it using colors of your choosing, and don't feel confined by having to stay inside the lines.

FIND OUT ABOUT...

People	Places	Potpourri
Amelia Earhart	Earth	$E = mc^2$
Wyatt Earp	East Germany	*E Pluribus Unum*
Albert Einstein	Edinburgh	Eclipse (solar or lunar)
George Eliot	Egypt	Entomology
Queen Elizabeth (I or II)	Eiffel Tower	Entrepreneurs
Duke Ellington	Ellis Island	ESP
Leif Ericson	Erie Canal	*Excalibur*
Euripides	Ethiopia	Extraterrestrials

WORDS

eagle	edge	error
earth	elbow	even
east	elk	exact

CHALLENGE WORDS

ebullient	egocentric	equinox
eccentric	electroencephalograph	et cetera
effigy	embryo	exacerbate

VINTON ©

HISTORY

The letter E comes from the Phoenician "He"—their consonant H. The Greeks reversed the Phoenician letter, renamed it "Epsilon," and used it as the vowel E. The Romans gave it the shape we know today.

PHOENICIAN	OLD HEBREW	EARLY GREEK	CLASSICAL GREEK

ETRUSCAN	EARLY LATIN	MODERN ROMAN

• •

"E" IN MORE ALPHABETS

MANUAL ALPHABET

SEMAPHORE

BRAILLE

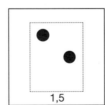

1,5

INTERNATIONAL FLAG CODE

MORSE CODE

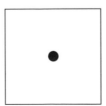

NATO CODE

Echo
(ECK-OH)

FUN FACTS

An F-stop is a camera lens aperture setting. The F means "focal length." Most newer cameras are automatic so you don't have to set the F-stop. F is the chemical symbol for the pale yellow gas Fluorine. It's also a note on the musical scale and the abbreviation for Fahrenheit.

PROJECT

Fracture a famous story. Rewrite it your way. Have it take place in a new period or setting. *Fit* yourself into the story as one of the characters or as a new character that everyone else must deal with. Have *fun!*

FIND OUT ABOUT...

People	Places	Potpourri
William Faulkner	Falkland Islands	Fables (Aesop's)
Ella Fitzgerald	Fiji	FBI
Henry Ford	Finland	Feminism
George Foreman	Florence	Fiestas
Anne Frank	Florida	Fingerprinting
Sigmund Freud	Fort Sumter	Fish
Robert Frost	Fort Worth	FM radio
Robert Fulton	France	Frankenstein

WORDS

face	family	first
fad	fence	flag
fake	fine	foot

CHALLENGE WORDS

facade	fastidious	flamboyant
Fahrenheit	fathom	fleece
famine	feign	fulcrum

"Tell me and I forget, teach me and I remember, involve me and I learn."

Benjamin Franklin

HISTORY

The letter F comes from the Phoenician "Waw." The early Greek alphabet had a letter called "Digamma" that eventually disappeared; the Romans used it to mean F. We borrowed it from the Romans unchanged.

PHOENICIAN	OLD HEBREW	EARLY GREEK	CLASSICAL GREEK

ETRUSCAN	EARLY LATIN	MODERN ROMAN

WHAT'S IN THE PICTURE?

Clockwise from top

Fish

Five

Fan

Fire hydrant

Frightened★

Fire

French Fries

Four

Fireflies

Frankenstein

"F" IN MORE ALPHABETS

MANUAL ALPHABET

SEMAPHORE

BRAILLE
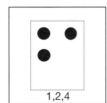

1,2,4

INTERNATIONAL FLAG CODE
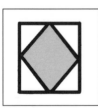

MORSE CODE

NATO CODE

Foxtrot (FOKS-TROT)

FRANKIE

4

G
g

FUN FACTS

A G is a unit of force equal to the force of gravity at the Earth's surface. If you are subjected to 3 G's in a jet, then you are experiencing 3 times the force that gravity would normally be exerting on your body. Astronauts and pilots of supersonic jets must be able to withstand high G's and still maintain consciousness and reasoning abilities. In slang, a "G-man" is a special agent of the FBI, and a "G-note" is a $1000 bill.

PROJECT

Glue a picture together in a "gnu" way. Take a photocopy (or multiples) of a picture, cut it up, and rearrange the parts to create a brand new image. Teacher faces work well—lots of laughs.

FIND OUT ABOUT...

People	Places	Potpourri
Galileo	Galápagos Islands	Galaxy
Indira Gandhi	Ganges River	Garfield the Cat
Mohandas Gandhi	Gettysburg	Gargoyles
Bill Gates	Gibraltar	Gerbils
Geronimo	Globe Theatre	G.I. Joe
Dizzy Gillespie	Grand Canyon	GNP
Nikki Giovanni	Great Britain	Goosebumps
Pancho Gonzales	Greenwich	Holy Grail

WORDS

gage	gear	glad
game	germ	goat
gang	give	grin

CHALLENGE WORDS

gaffe	genre	gibberish
garrulous	geodesic	grandeur
gazette	gesundheit	gyroscope

VINTON ©

HISTORY

The letter G comes from the Phoenician "Gimel," which meant "camel." The Greeks turned it around and named it "Gamma." The Romans used Gamma for both the G sound and the K sound. To eliminate confusion, they added a bar to the C and created the G we use today.

PHOENICIAN	OLD HEBREW	MODERN ROMAN
		Gg

WHAT'S IN THE PICTURE?

Clockwise from top

Galaxy (stars)

Goose or Gander

Go sign

Ghost

Garbage can

Globe

Gopher

Giddy★

Giraffe

Goat

"G" IN MORE ALPHABETS

MANUAL ALPHABET

SEMAPHORE

BRAILLE
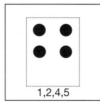

1,2,4,5

INTERNATIONAL FLAG CODE
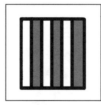

MORSE CODE

NATO CODE
Golf
(GOLF)

34

"The human mind, once stretched to a new idea, never goes back to its original dimensions."

Oliver Wendell Holmes

FUN FACTS

H is the chemical symbol for Hydrogen, a colorless, odorless gas. It is believed that hydrogen atoms make up about 90 percent of the universe. The H-bomb is a hydrogen bomb. In many Romance languages, the H is sometimes silent—as in the English word "honor."

PROJECT

Haiku. Write one or more poems using this ancient Japanese form: 3 unrhymed lines of 5, 7, and 5 syllables each.

> *This is not a good*
> *haiku, but it shows you where*
> *the syllables go.*

You might write about feelings, nature, the seasons, or anything you choose.

FIND OUT ABOUT...

People	Places	Potpourri
Alex Haley	Haiti	Helicopters
John Hancock	Hamburg	Hercules
Hannibal	Harpers Ferry	Hermit crabs
Helen of Troy	Havana	Hippies
Hiawatha	Himalayas	Holograms
Harry Houdini	Hollywood	Hubble Space Telescope
Huckleberry Finn	Hong Kong	Hurricanes
Zora Neale Hurston	Honolulu	Hypnosis

WORDS

habit	happy	history
hair	hawk	home
hand	help	hug

CHALLENGE WORDS

halcyon	harlequin	helix
haphazard	haughty	homogeneous
harbinger	helium	humanitarianism

HISTORY

The letter H comes from the Phoenician "Heth." The Greeks borrowed Heth and named it "Eta." Eta was used to stand for the H sound and later for E. The Romans borrowed it in its original Greek form, and we borrowed it from the Romans.

PHOENICIAN	OLD HEBREW	EARLY GREEK	CLASSICAL GREEK

ETRUSCAN	EARLY LATIN	MODERN ROMAN

WHAT'S IN THE PICTURE?

Clockwise from top

House

Heart

Honeycomb

Hateful★

Hippo

Hot dog

Hat

Hand

Horse

"H" IN MORE ALPHABETS

MANUAL ALPHABET

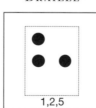

SEMAPHORE

BRAILLE

1,2,5

INTERNATIONAL FLAG CODE

MORSE CODE

●●●●

NATO CODE

Hotel
(HOH-TELL)

38

I

i

"It is better to die on your feet than to live on your knees."

Dolores Ibárruri

FUN FACTS

The letter I is a good example of a homonym—a word that has the same sound as another word but may be spelled differently and means something else. Consider "I" (me), "eye" (see), and "aye" ("aye-aye Captain!"). I is the chemical symbol for Iodine; it's also the shape of an I-beam. A small i means 1 in Roman numerals; in math, it stands for "imaginary unit"—the positive square root of negative 1.

PROJECT

Illustrate a famous quotation. Discuss and explain the author's meaning or portray what the quotation means to you personally.

FIND OUT ABOUT...

People	Places	Potpourri
Lee Iacocca	Indian Ocean	IBM
Dolores Ibárruri	Indonesia	Icarus
Henrik Ibsen	Iowa	Iguanas
Roy Innis	Iraq	Incas
Daniel K. Inouye	Israel	Infinity
Washington Irving	Istanbul	Internet
James B. Irwin	Ivory Coast	Invisible Man
Queen Isabella I	Iwo Jima	Ionosphere

WORDS

ice	igloo	index
idea	import	ink
idol	Inca	into

CHALLENGE WORDS

ichthyology	imbue	individualism
idiom	imperceptible	infinity
imaginative	incandescent	invertebrate

HISTORY

The letter I comes from the Phoenician "Yodh," which meant "hand" and stood for the Y sound, as in "toy." The Greeks took Yodh, turned it into "Iota," and used it for the vowel I. The Romans borrowed it from the Greeks and its shape has remained unchanged. The dot over the lowercase i came into use during the 11th century.

PHOENICIAN	EARLY GREEK	CLASSICAL GREEK
Ƨ	Ƨ	I

ETRUSCAN	EARLY LATIN	MODERN ROMAN
I	I	Ii

WHAT'S IN THE PICTURE?

Clockwise from top

Iguana

Infinity sign

Inchworm

Island

Icy★

Igloo

Iceberg

Insect

"I" IN MORE ALPHABETS

MANUAL ALPHABET

SEMAPHORE

BRAILLE

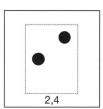

2,4

INTERNATIONAL FLAG CODE

MORSE CODE

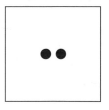

NATO CODE

India
(IN-DEE-AH)

J j

FUN FACTS

A jaywalker is not a set of legs on a J, but someone who crosses the street anywhere but at a crosswalk. A jaybird is another word for a jay, a bird of the crow family. The letter J is the abbreviation for "joule," a unit of electrical energy. A J-bar is a type of ski lift. And someone who's a "J.V." is a member of a junior varsity team.

PROJECT

Joke around. Write a funny monologue and try it out on an audience, just for laughs.

FIND OUT ABOUT...

People	Places	Potpourri
Andrew Jackson	Jacksonville	Jason and the Argonauts
Jesse Jackson	Jamaica	Jazz
Thomas Jefferson	Jamestown	Jellyfish
Dr. Jekyll	Japan	Jet lag
Joan of Arc	Jericho	Juggernaut
Lyndon Baines Johnson	Johannesburg	Jumping beans
Scott Joplin	Jordan River	Jurassic
Barbara Jordan	Jupiter	Jurisprudence

WORDS

jade	jazz	join
jam	jelly	jump
jar	jingle	jungle

CHALLENGE WORDS

jackal	jeopardize	jocular
jalapeño	jettison	judicious
jambalaya	jingoism	jujitsu

© VINTON

HISTORY

The letter J is a medieval transformation of the letter I. The Romans used I for both the sounds i ("bit") and y ("yet"). They didn't yet have the sound for J. During the Middle Ages, the I was kept as a vowel and a new letter, J, was added by attaching a tail. It wasn't until the middle of the 17th century that J appeared in English books. In English today, the J has a new sound ("judge").

● ●

WHAT'S IN THE PICTURE?

Clockwise from top

Jug

Jack-o'-lantern

Jam

Jeep

Jacks

Jolly★

Jet

Jack-in-the-box

"J" IN MORE ALPHABETS

MANUAL ALPHABET

SEMAPHORE

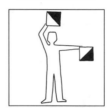

BRAILLE

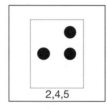

2,4,5

INTERNATIONAL FLAG CODE

MORSE CODE

NATO CODE

Juliet
(JEW-LEE-ETT)

K k

FUN FACTS

A karat—abbreviated as K—is a unit of measure for the fineness of gold. The higher the karat number, the purer the gold. 24K gold is pure gold; 12K gold is 50 percent pure. K is also the chemical symbol for Potassium. In slang, a K is $1000. In science, K stands for Kelvin, a unit of absolute temperature. In computer science, a KB is a kilobyte—1,000 bytes. In education, K means "kindergarten." And K2 is the official name of the world's second highest mountain, after Everest.

PROJECT

Killer phrases. Come up with phrases that stifle creativity. *Examples:* "It can't be done." "Don't even try." "What is THAT?" List as many as you can think of, then discuss and debate them. Why *shouldn't* you let them stand in your way?

FIND OUT ABOUT...

People	Places	Potpourri
Frida Kahlo	Kansas	Kangaroos
Helen Keller	Kenya	Kentucky Derby
John F. Kennedy	Khyber Pass	KGB
Captain Kidd	Kilimanjaro	Killer whales
Coretta Scott King	Kitty Hawk	Kinetic energy
Dr. Martin Luther King, Jr.	The Kremlin	King Kong
Ray Kroc	Krypton	Kites
Akira Kurosawa	Kuwait	Knights of the Round Table

WORDS

keep	kid	kiss
key	kind	knee
kick	king	know

CHALLENGE WORDS

kaleidoscope	kerosene	kindergarten
kangaroo	kilobyte	knucklehead
kayak	kilometer	koala

HISTORY

The letter K comes from the Phoenician "Kaph," which meant "hollow of the hand." The Greeks reversed it and called it "Kappa." The Romans borrowed it but used it very little; our K is taken from theirs.

PHOENICIAN	OLD HEBREW	EARLY GREEK	CLASSICAL GREEK
𐤊	𐤊	𐤊	Κ

ETRUSCAN	EARLY LATIN	MODERN ROMAN
𐌊	K	Kk

"K" IN MORE ALPHABETS

MANUAL ALPHABET

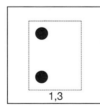

SEMAPHORE

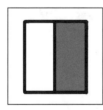

BRAILLE

1,3

INTERNATIONAL FLAG CODE

MORSE CODE

NATO CODE

Kilo
(KEY-LOH)

L l

FUN FACTS

L is one of many letters the Romans used to stand for numbers; in Roman numerals, L means 50. A small l is the abbreviation for "liter." It can also be used to mean "left" or, on clothing tags, "large."

PROJECT

Laugh! Try to find at least a little humor in everything. Learn to laugh at yourself. Get a book on cartooning and learn to draw funny characters.

FIND OUT ABOUT...

People	Places	Potpourri
Sir Lancelot	Labrador	La Brea Tar Pits
Lawrence of Arabia	Lake Victoria	Labyrinth
Le Corbusier	Las Vegas	Latitude and Longitude
Leadbelly (Huddie Ledbetter)	Lexington and Concord	Leopards
Spike Lee	Libya	Light year
Abraham Lincoln	London	Llamas
Anne Morrow Lindbergh	Louvre	Lucy (and the rest of the *Peanuts* gang)
Clare Boothe Luce	Luxembourg	*Lusitania*

WORDS

labor	land	light
lace	leaf	load
lamb	less	luck

CHALLENGE WORDS

labyrinth	lieutenant	loquacious
lackadaisical	limousine	lugubrious
legible	linoleum	luscious

"Most folks are about as happy as they make up their minds to be."

Abraham Lincoln

52

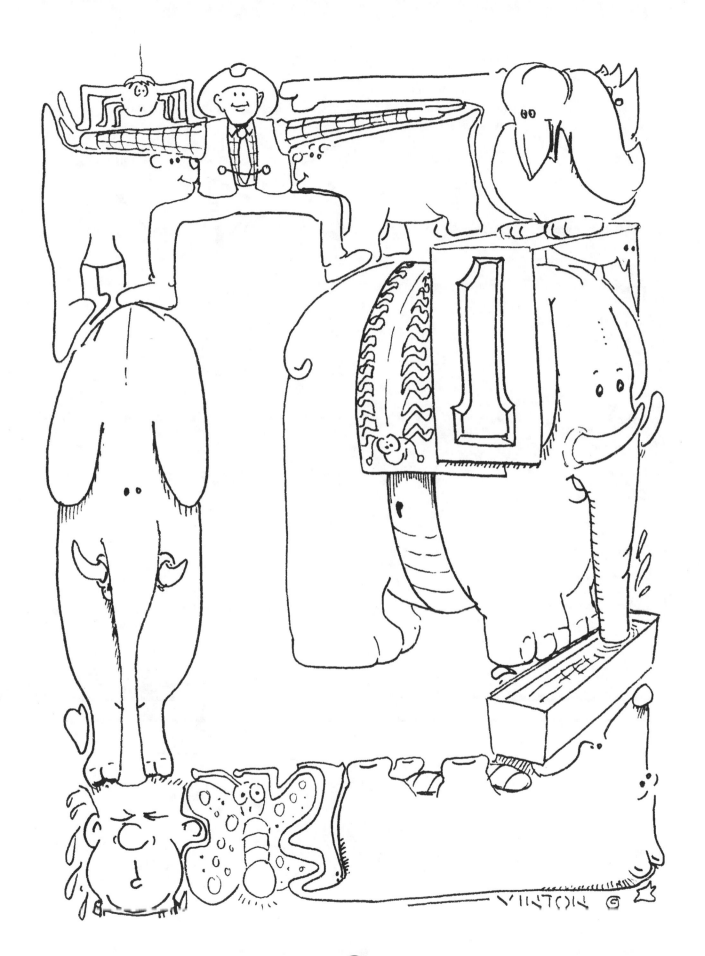

HISTORY

The letter L hasn't changed much over the centuries. It started out as the Phoenician letter "Lamadh." The Greeks made it into "Lambda," and the Romans gave it the shape we still use today.

PHOENICIAN	OLD HEBREW	EARLY GREEK	CLASSICAL GREEK
Ɩ	Ɩ	٦	∧

ETRUSCAN	EARLY LATIN	MODERN ROMAN
✔	Ɩ	LI

WHAT'S IN THE PICTURE?

Clockwise from top

Ladder

Lighthouse

In Love★

Lizard

Lawnmower

Lantern

Life preserver

Leaf with Lasso

"L" IN MORE ALPHABETS

MANUAL ALPHABET

SEMAPHORE

BRAILLE

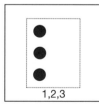

1,2,3

INTERNATIONAL FLAG CODE

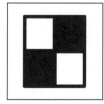

MORSE CODE

NATO CODE

Lima
(LEE-MAH)

"Don't put off till tomorrow what you can do today because if you enjoy it today, you can do it again tomorrow."

James Michener

FUN FACTS

M&M's—the bite-sized chocolate candies that "melt in your mouth, not in your hand"—were named for Forrest Mars and Bruce Murries, the people who invented them. M&M's were first sold in 1941; today, more than 50 *billion* are made each year. In Roman numerals, M means 1,000. The abbreviation m stands for "meter," and mm stands for "millimeter"—one thousandth of a meter.

PROJECT

Metamorphosize. To "metamorphosize" something means to transform its appearance or function. Draw an object in four stages: 1) real, 2) surreal, 3) semi-abstract, and 4) abstract. Which is the hardest to draw? Which is the most fun?

FIND OUT ABOUT...

People	Places	Potpourri
Douglas MacArthur	Machu Picchu	Magna Carta
Macbeth	Maginot Line	Manhattan Project
Malcolm X	Manhattan	M.A.S.H.
Nelson Mandela	Manitoba	Mason-Dixon Line
Mickey Mantle	Mars	Merlin
A.A. Milne	Mecca	Mickey Mouse
Carol Mosely-Braun	Mohave Desert	Murphy's Law
Mother Teresa	Morocco	Mythology

WORDS

made	man	mile
magic	maple	money
mall	mend	myth

CHALLENGE WORDS

magenta	mannequin	millimeter
magnificent	medieval	monosyllable
maharaja	megalomania	mythological

HISTORY

The Phoenician letter for M was "Mem," which meant "water." The Greeks renamed it "Mu" and turned it around. The Romans borrowed it and gave it the symmetrical form we know today.

PHOENICIAN	OLD HEBREW	EARLY GREEK	CLASSICAL GREEK

ETRUSCAN	EARLY LATIN	MODERN ROMAN

"M" IN MORE ALPHABETS

MANUAL ALPHABET

SEMAPHORE

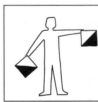

BRAILLE

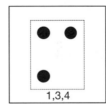

1,3,4

INTERNATIONAL FLAG CODE

MORSE CODE

NATO CODE

Mike
(MIKE)

WHAT'S IN THE PICTURE?

Clockwise from top

Moose

Musical Measure

Magnet

Microscope

Mouse with a Megaphone

Monogram

Mad★

Mushroom

Mummy

Moon

"When you do something you are proud of, praise yourself for it."

Mildred Newman

FUN FACTS

The letter N is used for many different abbreviations. In chemistry, N is the symbol for Nitrogen, the element that makes up nearly four-fifths of the air we breathe. N is also the symbol for Avogadro's Number—the number of molecules in one mole of a substance (about 6.02×10^{23})—and for Newton, a unit of force. A small n can mean a "neutron" or, in math, an "unknown number." N is also used to point North on maps.

PROJECT

Never say never. Put up a sign in your room that says, "CAN'T is a four-letter word! Don't use it here!" Make a list of three or more positive things you didn't do because you told yourself "I can't" (or someone else said "You can't"). Choose one you *can* do—and do it!

FIND OUT ABOUT...

People	Places	Potpourri
Ralph Nader	Nashville	NASA
Napoleon	Neptune	New York Marathon
Martina Navrátilová	Never-Never Land	Nightingales
Horatio Nelson	New Guinea	*1984* (the novel)
Pablo Neruda	Niagara Falls	Nostradamus
Sir Isaac Newton	Nile River	Nova
Florence Nightingale	Norfolk	Nuclear family
Jessye Norman	Notre Dame de Paris	Numismatics

WORDS

nail	neck	normal
name	next	nose
near	nice	number

CHALLENGE WORDS

naturalize	niche	non sequitur
Neanderthal	nocturnal	nucleus
nefarious	nomenclature	nutrition

HISTORY

The letter N comes from the Phoenician "Nun," which meant "fish." The Greeks renamed it "Nu" and flipped it. The Romans borrowed it and made it look the way it does today.

PHOENICIAN	OLD HEBREW	EARLY GREEK	CLASSICAL GREEK

ETRUSCAN	EARLY LATIN	MODERN ROMAN

WHAT'S IN THE PICTURE?

Clockwise from top

Night

Net

Nozzle

Nutcracker and Nut

Nervous★

Nest

Needle

Notes

Nine

"N" IN MORE ALPHABETS

MANUAL ALPHABET

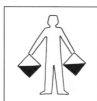

SEMAPHORE

BRAILLE

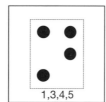

1,3,4,5

INTERNATIONAL FLAG CODE

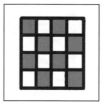

MORSE CODE

NATO CODE

November (NO-VEM-BER)

FUN FACTS

"O" is a word often used to express surprise or strong emotion ("O my goodness!") It's the most popular blood type in the world, and the chemical symbol for Oxygen. A small o is the symbol for "ohm," a unit of electrical resistance.

PROJECT

Oxymorons. An oxymoron is a combination of opposite or contradictory terms that kind of make sense. *Examples:* jumbo shrimp, pretty ugly. Come up with a list of oxymorons and illustrate them.

FIND OUT ABOUT...

People	Places	Potpourri
Annie Oakley	Ohio River	*Odyssey*
Sandra Day O'Connor	Okefenokee Swamp	OPEC
Eugene O'Neill	Oklahoma	Opossums
J. Robert Oppenheimer	Mt. Olympus	Orbit
George Orwell	Ontario	Ornithology
Osceola	Oregon Trail	Osmosis
Ovid	Ouangolodougou	Otters
Jesse Owens	Outer Mongolia	Ozone hole

WORDS

obey	olive	ooze
odd	once	orange
offer	only	owl

CHALLENGE WORDS

observatory	Olympic	orangutan
obtuse	omnivore	oscillate
official	operational	ovoid

"All animals are equal but some animals are more equal than others."

George Orwell

HISTORY

The letter O is basically the way it was when the Phoenicians invented it. The Greeks and the Romans kept it as is. We decided not to change a good thing.

PHOENICIAN

OLD HEBREW

EARLY GREEK

CLASSICAL GREEK

ETRUSCAN

EARLY LATIN

MODERN ROMAN

WHAT'S IN THE PICTURE?

Clockwise from top

Outer space

Otter

One

Ostrich in Overshoes

Obstinate★

Oar

Outlet

Owl

Octagon

Observatory

"O" IN MORE ALPHABETS

MANUAL ALPHABET

SEMAPHORE

BRAILLE
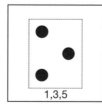

1,3,5

INTERNATIONAL FLAG CODE
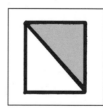

MORSE CODE
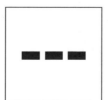

NATO CODE

Oscar
(OSS-CAH)

66

NO!

VINTON ©

FUN FACTS

In chemistry, P is the symbol for Phosphorus. In physics, it stands for "momentum" and also for "proton." In musical notation, it means "piano"—not the instrument, but instructions to play softly and quietly. In some words, the P itself is so quiet that it's absolutely silent (psychology, pneumonia).

PROJECT

Palindromes. A palindrome is a phrase that reads the same both forward and backward. *Example:* "Madam, I'm Adam." "Able was I ere I saw Elba." "A man, a plan, a canal: Panama." Create one or more palindromes. Or, if you can't come up with any, find some more famous palindromes.

FIND OUT ABOUT...

People	**Places**	**Potpourri**
Satchel Paige	Palestine	Parachute
Thomas Paine	Panama Canal	Periodic Table
Rosa Parks	Parthenon	Pinocchio
Louis Pasteur	Peru	Piranhas
Eva Perón	Phnom Penh	Polaris
Pocahontas	Pitcairn Island	Pony Express
Marco Polo	Pluto	Pop Art
General Colin Powell	Puerto Rico	Pyramids

WORDS

pack	pen	point
pay	pick	power
pear	pizza	price

CHALLENGE WORDS

parenthesis	phantom	popularity
pentagon	phosphorus	precipitation
periodic	piranha	premiere

"Don't look back. Someone might be gaining on you."

Satchel Paige

HISTORY

The letter P comes from the Phoenician "Pe," which meant "month." The Greeks turned it around and renamed it "Pi." The Romans closed the loop and gave us the P we use today.

PHOENICIAN	OLD HEBREW	EARLY GREEK	CLASSICAL GREEK
1	7	ʔ	Π

ETRUSCAN	EARLY LATIN	MODERN ROMAN
ʔ	Γ	Pp

WHAT'S IN THE PICTURE?

Clockwise from top

Polar bear

Pulley

Plate (home)

Parrot

Panda

Pyramid

Pain★

Palette

Paintbrush

Pear

Penguin with a Popsicle

"P" IN MORE ALPHABETS

MANUAL ALPHABET

SEMAPHORE

BRAILLE

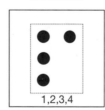

1,2,3,4

INTERNATIONAL FLAG CODE

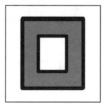

MORSE CODE

NATO CODE

Papa
(PAH-PAH)

Q q

FUN FACTS

The letter Q is the second to *least* used letter in the alphabet. In physics, it's the symbol for "charge." Queue (pronounced just like Q, but with a lot more letters) is a word that means a line of waiting people or vehicles—or a pigtail.

PROJECT

Quantum thinking. Make BIG jumps in thinking to answer questions. (Why is the sky blue? Why is blue blue?) Question everything; use opposing viewpoints to gain insights. List five BIG questions you're curious about and try to find the answers.

FIND OUT ABOUT...

People	Places	Potpourri
Muammar al Qaddafi	Qatar	Quails
Quakers	Quaker Valley	Quantum leap
Salvatore Quasimodo	Quebec	Quarantine
Dan Quayle	Queens	Quarks
Quecha Indians	Queensland	Quartet
Ellery Queen	Quetzalcoatl	Quasars
Anna Quindlen	Quito	Quicksand
Quintilian	Qumran	Quinine

WORDS

quack	queen	quit
quail	quest	quiz
quart	quick	quote

CHALLENGE WORDS

quadrant	questionable	quintuplets
qualification	quiescent	quotation
querulous	quintessential	quotient

HISTORY

The letter Q comes from the Phoenician "Qoph," which meant "monkey." The Greeks at first adopted it as "Quoppa" but had no real use for it. The Romans took it over and joined it with U to form the "kw" sound, and that's how we use it today.

PHOENICIAN

OLD HEBREW

EARLY GREEK

ETRUSCAN

EARLY LATIN

MODERN ROMAN

WHAT'S IN THE PICTURE?

Clockwise from top

Quill

Quack

Quarter

Question mark

Cue (sounds like "Q")

Queen

Quivering Quiver

Quizzical★

"Q" IN MORE ALPHABETS

MANUAL ALPHABET

SEMAPHORE
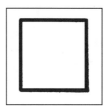

BRAILLE
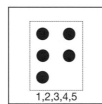
1,2,3,4,5

INTERNATIONAL FLAG CODE
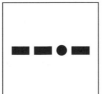

MORSE CODE

NATO CODE

Quebec (KEY-BECK)

R r

"Freedom is a hard-bought thing."
Paul Robeson

FUN FACTS

Have you ever wondered what "R.S.V.P." means on an invitation? It's the acronym for the French phrase *répondez s'il vous plait*—"please reply." In sports, an "RP" is a relief pitcher. In movies, an R rating means "under 17 not allowed unless accompanied by parent or guardian." In science, R is the symbol for Roentgen, a unit of radiation exposure. In chess, R means "rook."

PROJECT

Rewrite a famous speech. Take any well-known oration and put it in different words, or bend it and fracture it to create a new meaning. *Example:* "Four score and seven years ago, our forefathers . . ." might turn into "Eighty or so years back, gramps and his crew . . . ."

FIND OUT ABOUT...

People	Places	Potpourri
Ronald Reagan	Red Sea	Raccoons
Rembrandt	Reno	RAF
Paul Revere	Rhine River	Reconstruction
Sally Ride	Rhode Island	Redwoods
Paul Robeson	Rhodesia	Rites of passage
Robin Hood	Richmond	Rockets
Babe Ruth	Rio de Janeiro	Rosetta stone
Wilma Rudolph	Romania	Rumpelstiltskin

WORDS

rabbit	rain	right
race	read	root
radio	rely	rust

CHALLENGE WORDS

ramification	reciprocal	ricochet
rapscallion	recognition	roughage
raucous	reminiscent	rutabaga

HISTORY

The letter R comes from the Phoenician "Resh," which meant "head." The Greeks borrowed it and called it "Rho." Later the Romans added a diagonal tail to distinguish it from their own P. We use that form of R today.

PHOENICIAN	OLD HEBREW	EARLY GREEK	CLASSICAL GREEK
4	9	◁	P

ETRUSCAN	EARLY LATIN	MODERN ROMAN
4	P	Rr

WHAT'S IN THE PICTURE?

Clockwise from top

Rhinoceros

Rook

Rain

Rabbit

Rolling pin

Reflecting★

Racquet

Ricochet

Rope

"R" IN MORE ALPHABETS

MANUAL ALPHABET
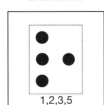

SEMAPHORE
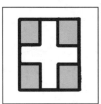

BRAILLE

1,2,3,5

INTERNATIONAL FLAG CODE
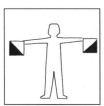

MORSE CODE

NATO CODE
Romeo (ROW-ME-OH)

"Creation is everything you do. Make something."

Ntozake Shange

FUN FACTS

The letter S has many uses. It's the chemical symbol for Sulfur and the cartographic symbol for South. It forms the plural and possessive of most nouns and is the short form of "is" and other words in contractions. A small s stands for "stere," another word for one cubic meter.

PROJECT

Shower power! Many great ideas and inventions are conceived in the shower, in the bath, on the beach, or other places when the brain is at rest. Take some time to *stop* using your conscious mind and rely on your *subconscious* to work. It's also a great *stress-beater.*

FIND OUT ABOUT...

People	Places	Potpourri
Sacajawea	Sahara	Saint Elmo's Fire
Anwar Sadat	Saturn	Satellites
Andrei Sakharov	Seattle	Scotland Yard
Carl Sandburg	Sesame Street	Scrooge McDuck
Dr. Seuss	Sherwood Forest	Silent films
William Shakespeare	Siberia	Skunks
Ntozake Shange	Singapore	Sonic boom
Margaret Chase Smith	Stonehenge	Superconductor

WORDS

sad	school	second
same	scout	sell
save	seal	sign

CHALLENGE WORDS

sabbatical	seismograph	soliloquy
sardonic	sequester	stethoscope
scapula	slough	subtlety

HISTORY

The letter S comes from the Phoenician "Shin," which meant "tooth." The Phoenicians sounded it like "sh." The Greeks borrowed it, changed its shape, and sounded it like "s." When the Romans borrowed it, they kept the sharp corners at first but later rounded them into the S we know today.

PHOENICIAN	OLD HEBREW	EARLY GREEK	CLASSICAL GREEK

ETRUSCAN	EARLY LATIN	MODERN ROMAN
		Ss

"S" IN MORE ALPHABETS

MANUAL ALPHABET

SEMAPHORE

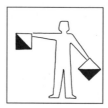

BRAILLE

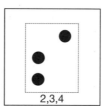

2,3,4

INTERNATIONAL FLAG CODE

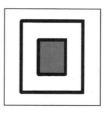

MORSE CODE

NATO CODE

Sierra
(SEE-AIR-RAH)

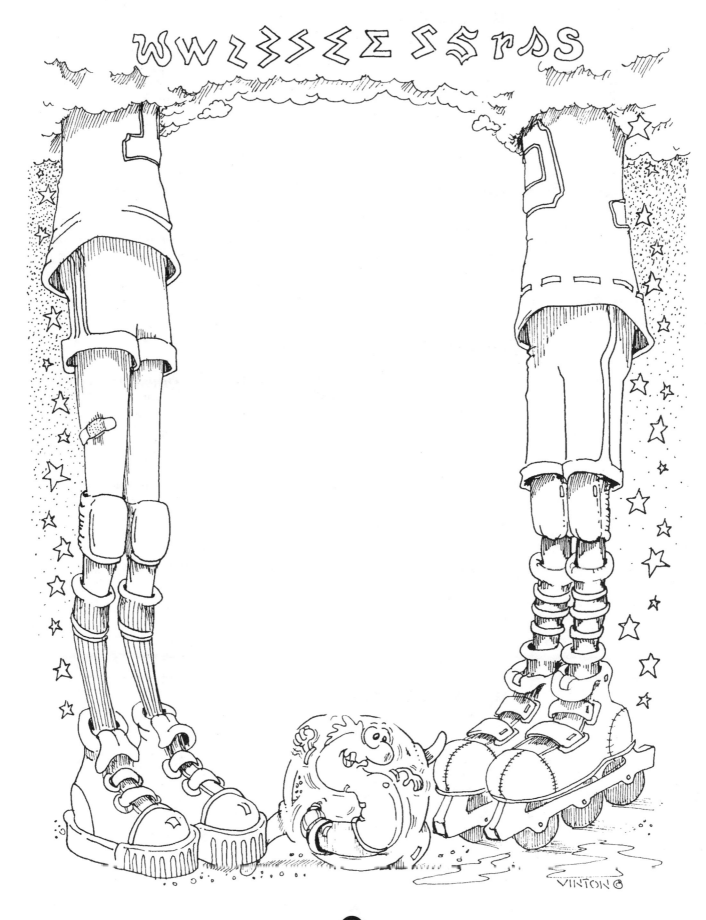

"It is never
too late to
give up our
Prejudices."
Henry David
Thoreau

FUN FACTS

When something "fits to a T," it's a perfect fit. T is the abbreviation for "temperature" and also for "troy weight." A T-bone is a kind of steak, and it's also slang for "trombone." In sports, a "TD" is a touchdown and a "TKO" is a technical knockout. We all have at least one T-shirt . . . and we could all use more TLC (tender loving care). In the phrase "T minus 10 and counting," the T stands for "time."

PROJECT

Tête-à-tête. This French phrase means "face-to-face." Go face-to-face with a friend or classmate and make contour drawings of each other. Contour drawings are all "line" with no shading or sketching. They are fun and easy to learn and do; many artists use them to develop characteristics quickly. Keep your pencil on the paper and draw what your eye sees, not what your brain tells you.

FIND OUT ABOUT...

People	Places	Potpourri
Mildred D. Taylor	Tahiti	Tarzan
Tchaikovsky	Tanzania	Telepathy
Tecumseh	Tehran	Tigers
Margaret Thatcher	Thailand	*Titanic*
Henry David Thoreau	Three Mile Island	Totem poles
Jim Thorpe	Tibet	Trail of Tears
Bishop Desmond Tutu	Timbuktu	Trilobites
Mark Twain	Tin Pan Alley	Trojan Horse

WORDS

table	tell	top
take	tennis	trap
tea	thick	tuba

CHALLENGE WORDS

taciturn	timpani	triumvirate
tenacity	tolerance	tsetse fly
therapeutic	tranquillity	tyrannosaurus

HISTORY

The letter T comes from the Phoenician "Taw," which looked like an X and meant "mark." The Greeks borrowed it, turned it around, and renamed it "Tau." The Romans borrowed Tau from the Greeks and kept it unchanged.

PHOENICIAN	OLD HEBREW	EARLY GREEK	CLASSICAL GREEK

ETRUSCAN	EARLY LATIN	MODERN ROMAN

WHAT'S IN THE PICTURE?

Clockwise from top

Truck

Toucan

T-square

Top hat

Telescope

Turtle

Tough★

Teddy bear

Ten

"T" IN MORE ALPHABETS

MANUAL ALPHABET

SEMAPHORE

BRAILLE

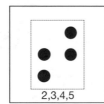

2,3,4,5

INTERNATIONAL FLAG CODE

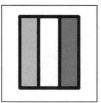

MORSE CODE

NATO CODE

Tango
(TAN-GO)

"It is our
responsibil-
ities, not
ourselves,
that we
should take
seriously."

Peter Ustinov

FUN FACTS

The term "U-Boat"—used to describe German submarines—comes from *unterseeboot,* the German for "undersea boat." A U-turn sends you back the way you came from. In chemistry, U is the abbreviation for Uranium. It's also the abbreviation for "university." UV light is ultraviolet light.

PROJECT

Unlimited thinking. The sky is no longer the limit! Ask questions. Question answers and results. Brainstorm. Think creatively. Write about or draw an "unlimited thinking" solution to a problem or challenge you're facing.

FIND OUT ABOUT...

People	Places	Potpourri
Stewart Udall	Uffizi Palace	UFOs
Ulysses	Uganda	Ukulele
Uncas	Ukraine	UN
Uncle Remus	Ulster	Uncle Sam
Sigrid Undset	United Arab Emirates	Underground Railroad
Johnny Unitas	Uranus	UNICEF
John Updike	Utopia	Unicorn
Maurice Utrillo	Uxmal	Ursa Major (and Minor)

WORDS

ugly	unfair	urn
uncle	unite	use
under	upbeat	usual

CHALLENGE WORDS

ubiquitous	unanimity	uproarious
ultimate	unctuous	urbane
ultraviolet	undulate	usurp

HISTORY

The Phoenician alphabet ended with T. The letters U, V, W, and Y are all relatively new. The U we know today can be traced back to the Phoenician "Waw," the Greek "Digamma" (ancestor of our F), and the Greek "Upsilon." The Romans took Upsilon and used for the U, V, and W sounds.

EARLY
GREEK

CLASSICAL
GREEK

ETRUSCAN

EARLY
LATIN

MODERN
ROMAN

"U" IN MORE ALPHABETS

MANUAL ALPHABET

SEMAPHORE

BRAILLE

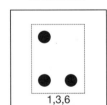

1,3,6

INTERNATIONAL FLAG CODE

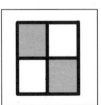

MORSE CODE

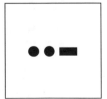

NATO CODE

Uniform
(YOU-NEE-
FORM)

WHAT'S
IN THE
PICTURE?

*Clockwise
from top*

United States

Umbrella

Unicorn

Unconscious★

Upside-down U

Unicycle

Urn

Up

V

FUN FACTS

A "V.I.P." is a Very Important Person. In chemistry, V is the symbol for Vanadium; in electricity, it's the symbol for "potential." In Roman numerals, a small v means 5.

PROJECT

Videotape a vision. Write a story, write the dialogue, figure out the parts, and videotape your vision. Produce your own play for others to see.

FIND OUT ABOUT...

People	Places	Potpourri
Vincent van Gogh	Valhalla	Vacuum
Sarah Vaughan	Valley Forge	Valentine's Day
Jules Verne	Vancouver	Vampire bats
Queen Victoria	Vatican City	Van Allen Belts
Pancho Villa	Venezuela	Ventriloquism
Virgil	Venus	Voice of America
Antonio Vivaldi	Vietnam	Volleyball
Werner Von Braun	Virginia	*Voyager* Program

WORDS

value	verb	video
van	very	volt
vein	veto	vote

CHALLENGE WORDS

vacuum	vaudeville	vitreous
vagabond	vegetarian	voluminous
variegated	vicissitude	voyager

"It is for you to discover yourself in a world where, alone and free, you may dream the possible dream."

Diana Vreeland

92

HISTORY

The letter V is a changed form of the letter U, which was adapted from the Greek "Upsilon." The Romans used V to stand for U, V, and W. Our modern printed V is modeled after the angular shape of the Roman letter. In English, the letters U and V were used interchangeably until the 17th century.

MODERN
ROMAN

WHAT'S IN THE PICTURE?

Clockwise from top

Vacuum cleaner

Vest

Vase

Vulture

Vicious★

Vise

Violin

Veins on a leaf

V-8

Vane (weather)

"V" IN MORE ALPHABETS

MANUAL ALPHABET

SEMAPHORE

BRAILLE

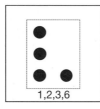

1,2,3,6

INTERNATIONAL FLAG CODE

MORSE CODE

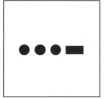

NATO CODE

Victor
(VIK-TAH)

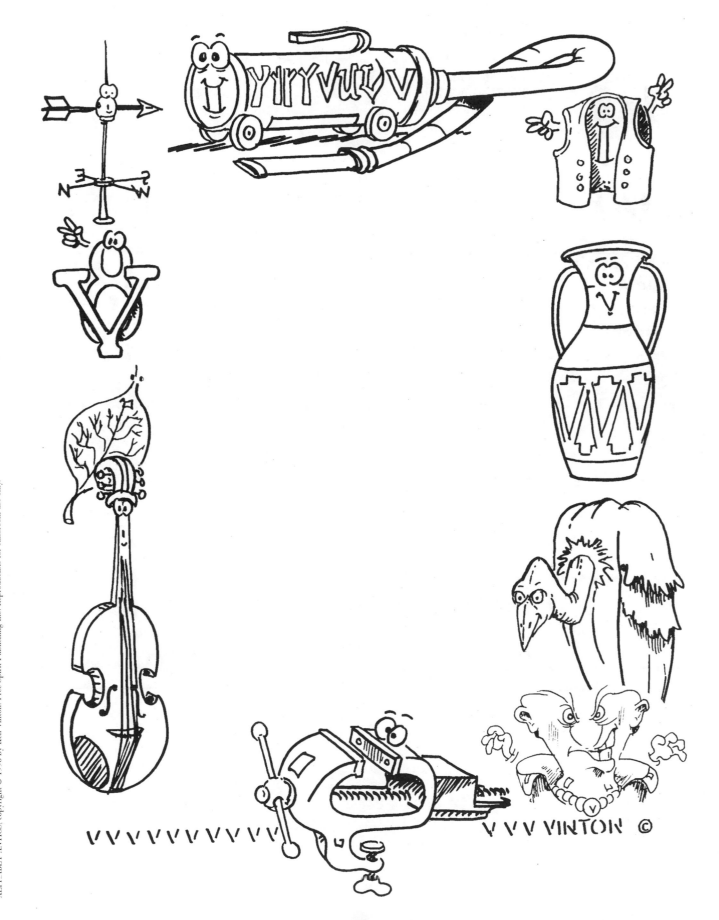

VVVVVVVVVVVV   V VV VINTON ©

"If art doesn't make us better, then what on earth is it for?"

Alice Walker

FUN FACTS

In chemistry, W is the symbol for Tungsten. In electricity, it's the symbol for watt. On a map, it means West. Paired, WW stands for "World War"—as in WWI and WWII.

PROJECT

Write a story of about 150 words using only one-syllable words. This can be fun and interesting. Maintain a theme or character.

FIND OUT ABOUT...

People	Places	Potpourri
Lech Walesa	Walden Pond	Washington Monument
Alice Walker	Wall Street	Watergate
Barbara Walters	Warsaw	Whales
Earl Warren	West Indies	White House
Booker T. Washington	Westminster Abbey	Windmills
Noah Webster	Windsor Castle	Winnie-the-Pooh
Orson Welles	Woodstock	World Series
The Wright Brothers	Wyoming	WPA

WORDS

wacky	water	will
wagon	went	with
wait	wheel	worn

CHALLENGE WORDS

watershed	wholesome	wondrous
weightless	witticism	wrestler
whimsical	wizened	writhe

VINTON

W

HISTORY

The W was a late arrival to our alphabet. Like the V, it originally came from the Greek "Upsilon." At first the Romans used V to stand for U, V, and W. It wasn't until much later that they realized the need to separate the sound. They placed two U's together (doubling the U's) and called the new letter W.

MODERN
ROMAN

WHAT'S IN THE PICTURE?

Clockwise from top

Walrus

Wasp

Windmill

Whistle

Wishbone

Whale

Worry★

Wrench

Wheel

Web

"W" IN MORE ALPHABETS

MANUAL ALPHABET

SEMAPHORE

BRAILLE

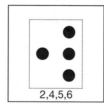

2,4,5,6

INTERNATIONAL FLAG CODE

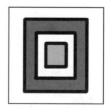

MORSE CODE

NATO CODE

Whiskey
(WISS-KEY)

"It takes
a wise man
to recognize
a wise man."

Xenophanes

FUN FACTS

People who were unable to sign their names often used an X as their signature. In movies, an X rating means that "no one under age 17 is admitted." In Roman numerals, X means 10. An X ray is a photograph taken with a stream of high-energy photons. And if you don't like these facts about the letter X, you can X them out.

PROJECT

X-er-size yer opshun two mspel. Take a famous quote and misspell every word you can. Mark Twain once said that he had no respect for anyone who could spell a word only one way. (You might find that this x-er-size helps to improve your spelling.)

FIND OUT ABOUT...

People	**Places**	**Potpourri**
The X-Men	Xanadu	X chromosome
Xenocrates	Xanthus	X ray
Xenophanes	Xenia	Xenophobia
Xenophon	Xi River	Xerography
Xerxes I	Xiamen	Xylem
Xhosa tribes	Xingu Port	Xylene
Ximénes	Xinjiang	Xylophone
Xuanzang	Lake Xochimilco	XYZ Affair

CHALLENGE WORDS

xebec	xenon	xylene
xenia	xerography	xylography
xenolith	xylem	xylophone

HISTORY

The letter X comes indirectly from the Phoenician "Samekh," which meant "fish" and stood for the "s" sound. The Greeks borrowed the Phoenician letter, called it "Xi," and gave it the "ks" sound. Later they changed it again, keeping the Xi name but simplifying the form to X. The X we use today is the Roman version.

EARLY GREEK

CLASSICAL GREEK

EARLY LATIN

MODERN ROMAN

WHAT'S IN THE PICTURE?

Clockwise from top

Xylophone

Symbol for female (females have two X chromosomes)

"X"cited★

X ray

Hugs & kisses

X files

Xmas tree

Xenon

X marks the spot

Planet X

"X" IN MORE ALPHABETS

MANUAL ALPHABET

SEMAPHORE

BRAILLE
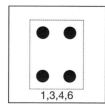
1,3,4,6

INTERNATIONAL FLAG CODE
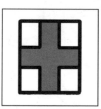

MORSE CODE

NATO CODE
X ray
(ECKS-RAY)

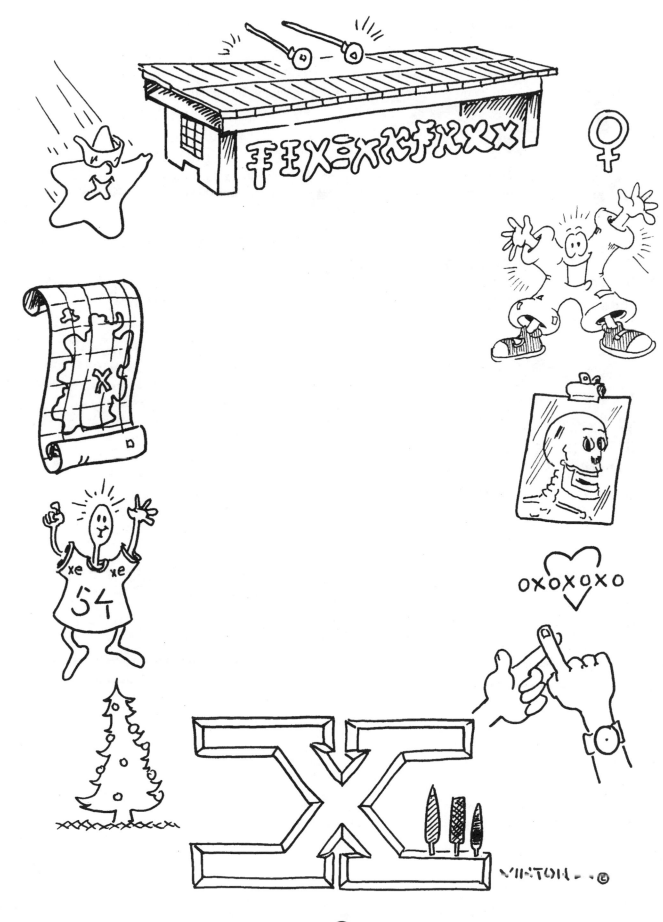

"Museums and galleries are for people. Children need to grow up in them. Art can give you excitement and energy."

Reva Yares

FUN FACTS

The Y chromosome determines gender. Females have two X chromosomes; males have both an X and a Y. In chemistry, Y is the symbol for Yttrium. Y can also stand for "yeoman," a petty officer in the U.S. Navy.

PROJECT

Yodels and yo-yos. Do you know how to yodel? Can you do yo-yo tricks? If not, pick one of these skills to learn. If you can yodel or do yo-yo tricks (or both), offer to teach someone else. Or choose another skill you'd like to learn.

FIND OUT ABOUT...

People	Places	Potpourri
Yashiro Yamashita	Yalta	Y chromosome
Chuck Yeager	Yangtze River	Yaks
William Butler Yeats	Yellowstone	"Yankee Doodle"
Boris Yeltsin	Yemen	Yankees
Yevgeny Yevtushenko	Yorktown	Yellow jackets
Andrew Young	Yosemite	Yellow journalism
Brigham Young	Yucatan	YMCA/YWCA
Cy Young	Yugoslavia	Yodeling

WORDS

yard	year	yield
yarn	yellow	your
yawn	yet	yummy

CHALLENGE WORDS

yahoo	yesterday	youngster
yearling	yogurt	youthful
yeoman	yonder	yucca

HISTORY

Like the V and the W, the letter Y is also related to U. The Greek letter "Upsilon" had two forms, Y and V. The Romans chose the first, Y, and used it as a U. By medieval times, Y was used for the sounds "i" and "y." Even today, our Y can have two sounds—as in "silly" or "sly."

MODERN
ROMAN

Yy

WHAT'S IN THE PICTURE?

Clockwise from top

Yacht

Yellow jacket

Yolk

Yardstick with Yarn

Yakking Yak wearing a Yoke

Yawn★

Yell

Symbol for male (males have a Y chromosome)

Yo-Yo

Year

"Y" IN MORE ALPHABETS

MANUAL ALPHABET

SEMAPHORE

BRAILLE

1,3,4,5,6

INTERNATIONAL FLAG CODE

MORSE CODE

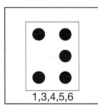

NATO CODE

Yankee
(YANG-KEY)

Z z

FUN FACTS

Z is the least used letter in the English alphabet. It might appear more often in chemical and mathematical equations than it does in words, since it's the symbol for Atomic Number and also for "impedance," a measure of opposition to flow in an AC current. Zowie!

PROJECT

Zero (zip) to Zenith. Compare the opposites of anything. *Examples:* black to white, red to green, Death Valley to Mount Everest, Hydrogen (atomic weight 1) to Unununium (atomic weight 272), E (most used letter) to Z (least used letter). When do we strive for the *most* of something? The *least* of something?

FIND OUT ABOUT...

People	Places	Potpourri
Babe Didrikson Zaharias	Zaire	Zebra
Darryl F. Zanuck	Zambia	Zeppelin
Emiliano Zapata	Zamezi River	Zero Population Growth
Zapotec Indians	Zanzibar	Ziggurat
Zhou Enlai	Zimbabwe	Zither
Zoroaster	Zion National Park	Zodiac
Zorro	Zululand	Zoology
Pinchas Zukerman	Zurich	Zoos

WORDS

zany	zenith	zip
zeal	zero	zone
zebra	zest	zoom

CHALLENGE WORDS

zealous	zodiac	zucchini
zephyr	zombie	zydeco
zirconium	zoological	zygote

HISTORY

The letter Z has not changed much in shape or sound usage over the years. The Phoenicians called it "Zayin," the Greeks renamed it "Zeta," and the Romans borrowed it, at first so they could translate Greek. We borrowed it from the Romans and zat's zat!

PHOENICIAN

EARLY GREEK

CLASSICAL GREEK

MODERN ROMAN

WHAT'S IN THE PICTURE?

Clockwise from top

Zeppelin

Zorro's mark

Zodiac

Zany★

Zig-Zag

Zero

Zipper

Zebu (snoring)

Zucchini

Zebra

"Z" IN MORE ALPHABETS

MANUAL ALPHABET

SEMAPHORE

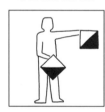

BRAILLE

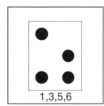

1,3,5,6

INTERNATIONAL FLAG CODE

MORSE CODE

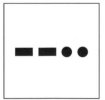

NATO CODE

Zulu
(ZOO-LOO)

MIKE · OSCAR · ROMEO · ECHO

MORE ALPHABETS

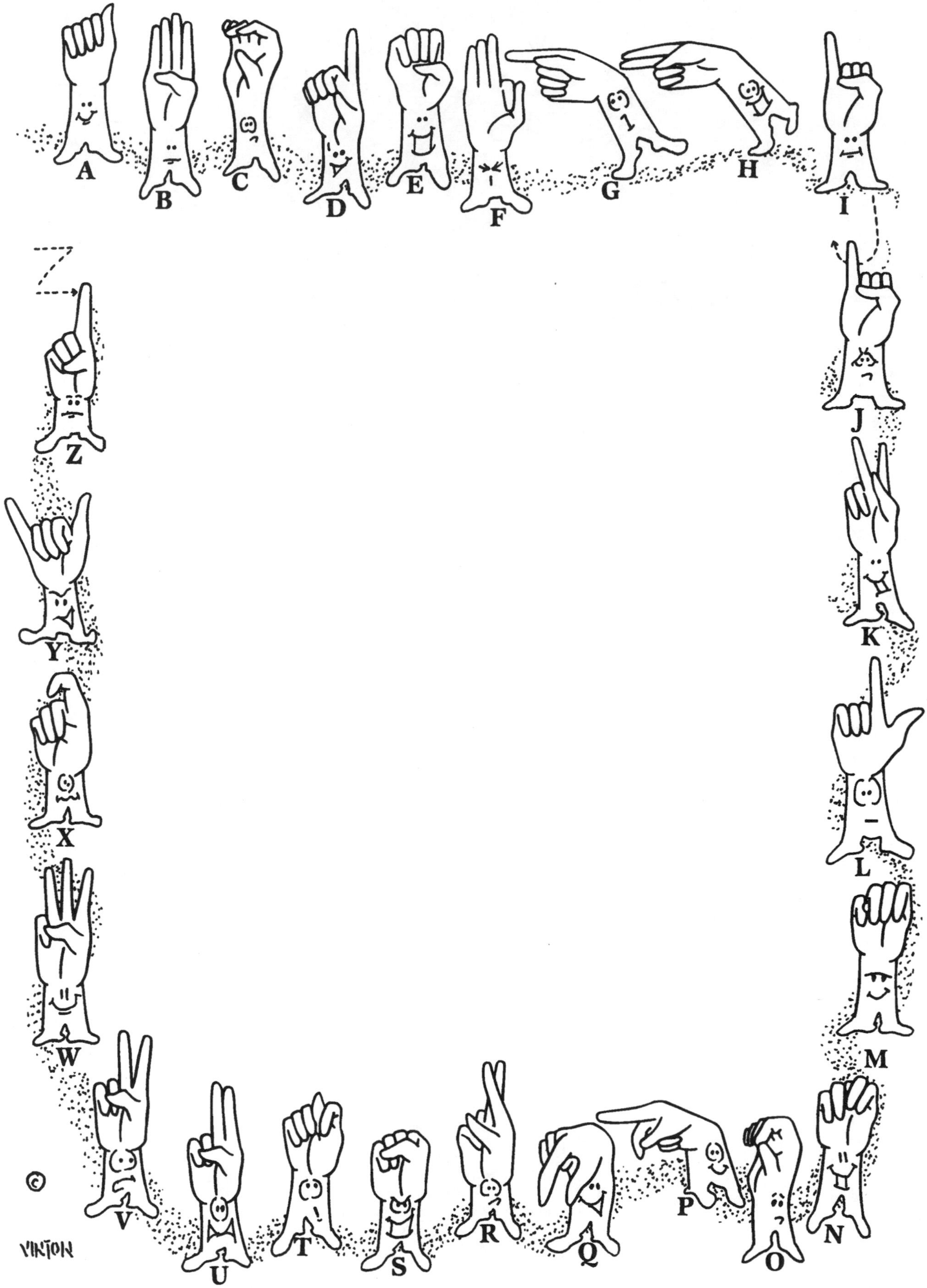
A B C D E F G H I
J K L M N
O P Q R S T U V
W X Y Z
©
VINTON

BRAILLE ALPHABET ★

A Braille cell has six dots.

The dots are numbered as follows:

```
1 ●  ● 4
2 ●  ● 5
3 ●  ● 6
```

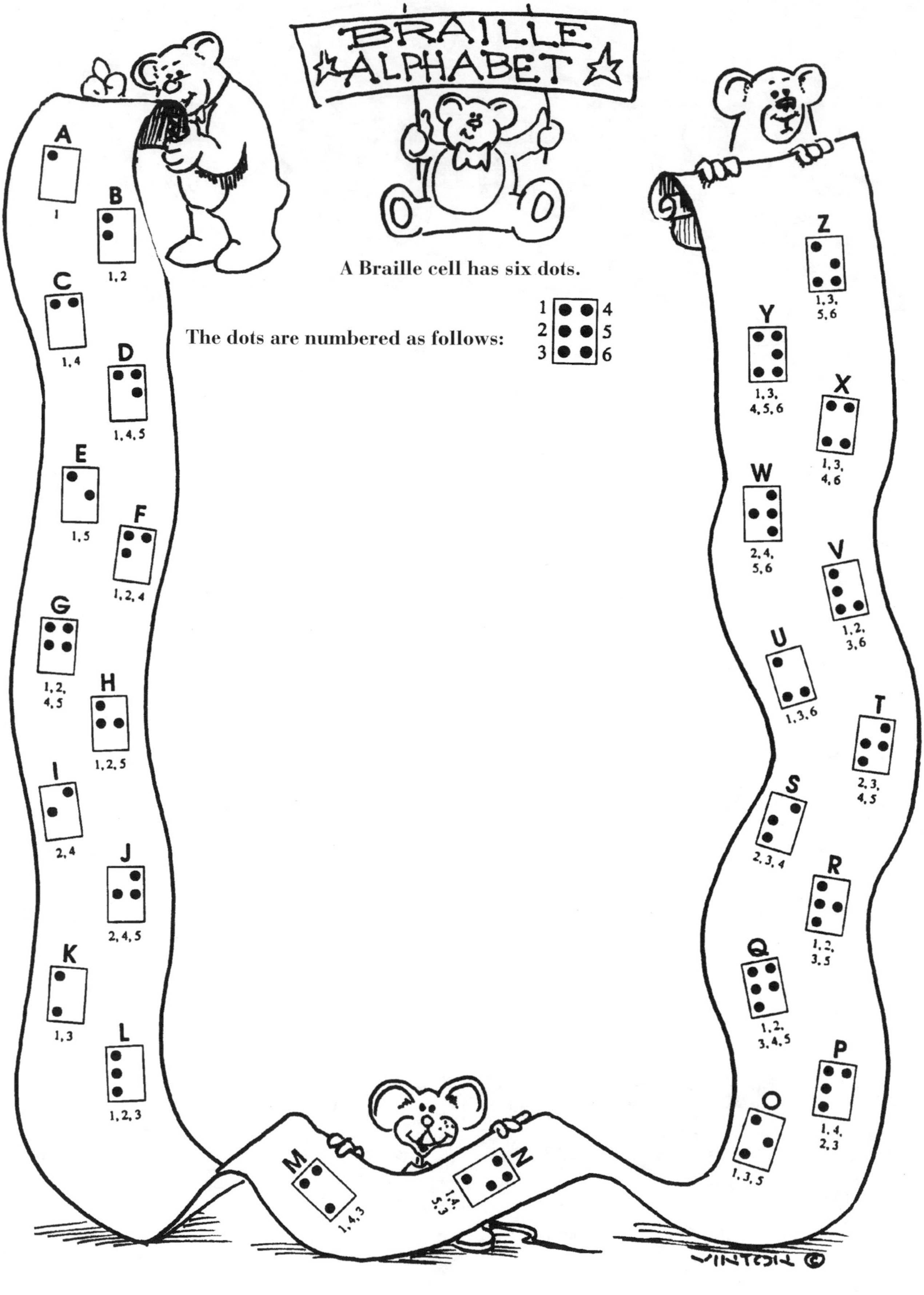

A — 1

B — 1, 2

C — 1, 4

D — 1, 4, 5

E — 1, 5

F — 1, 2, 4

G — 1, 2, 4, 5

H — 1, 2, 5

I — 2, 4

J — 2, 4, 5

K — 1, 3

L — 1, 2, 3

M — 1, 4, 3

N — 1, 4, 5, 3

O — 1, 3, 5

P — 1, 4, 2, 3

Q — 1, 2, 3, 4, 5

R — 1, 2, 3, 5

S — 2, 3, 4

T — 2, 3, 4, 5

U — 1, 3, 6

V — 1, 2, 3, 6

W — 2, 4, 5, 6

X — 1, 3, 4, 6

Y — 1, 3, 4, 5, 6

Z — 1, 3, 5, 6

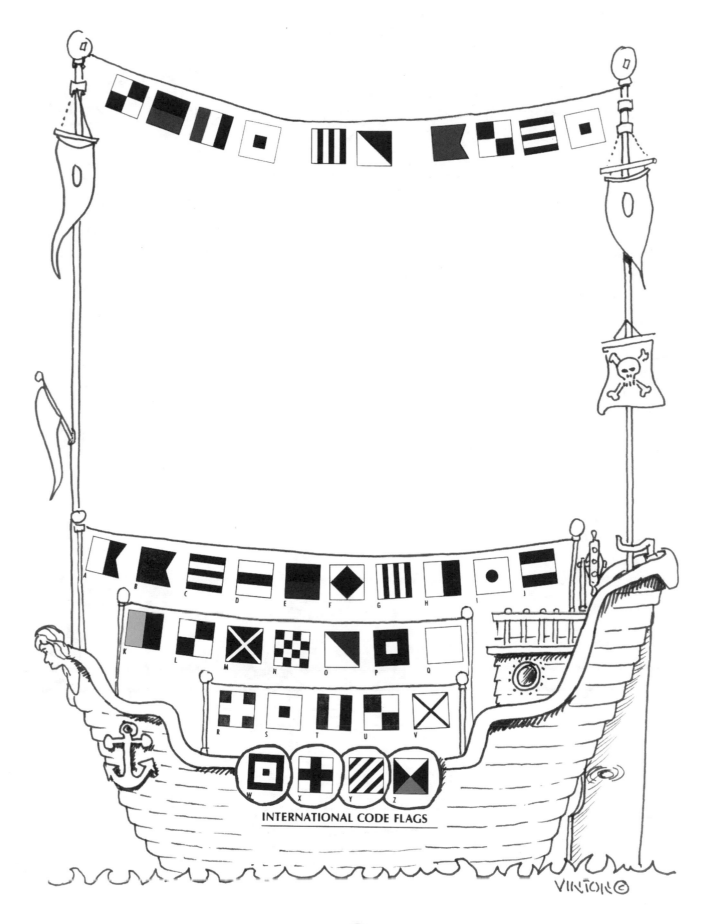

INTERNATIONAL CODE FLAGS

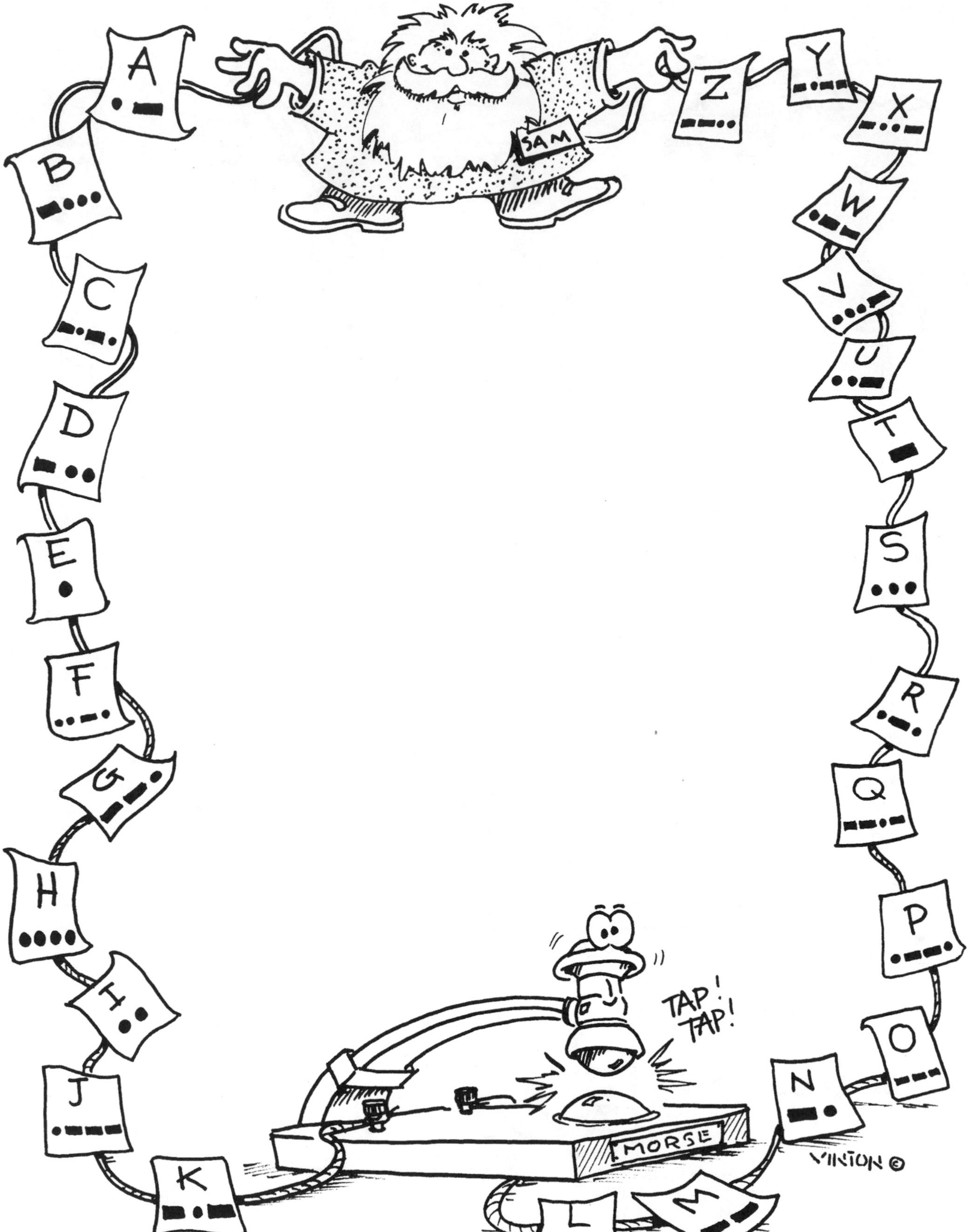
SAM
A
B
C
D
E
F
G
H
I
J
K
L
M
N
O
P
Q
R
S
T
U
V
W
X
Y
Z
TAP! TAP!
MORSE
VINTON ©

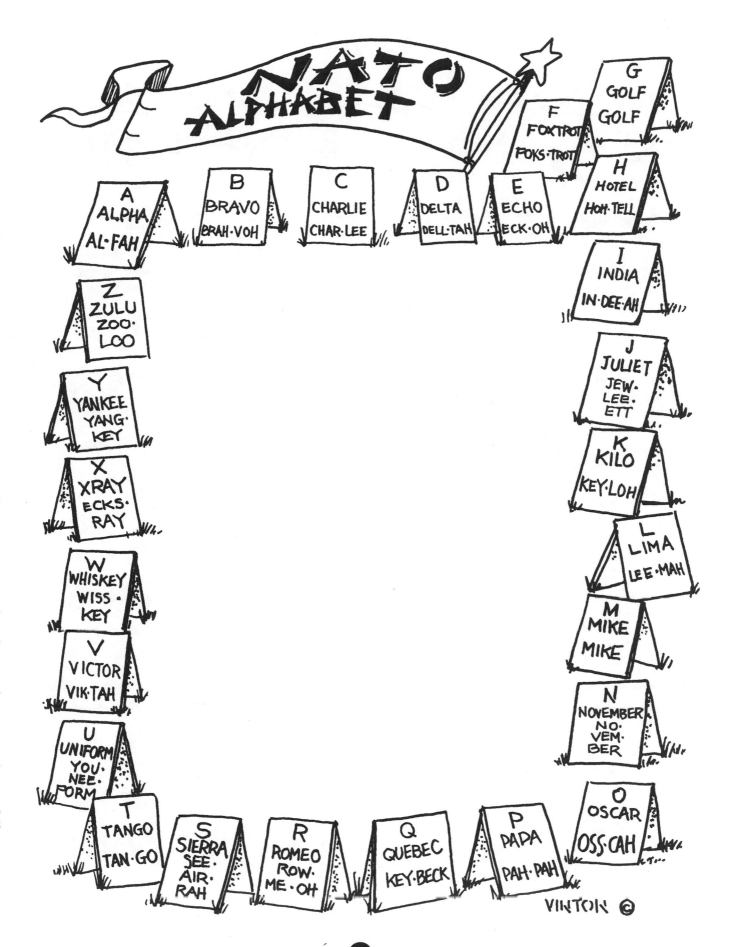

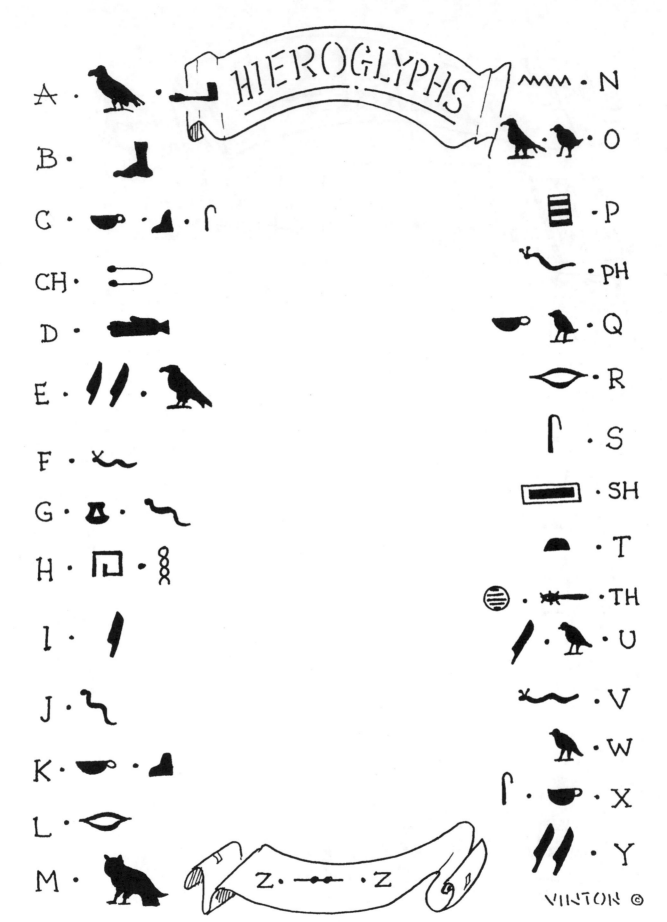

HIEROGLYPHS

VINTON ©

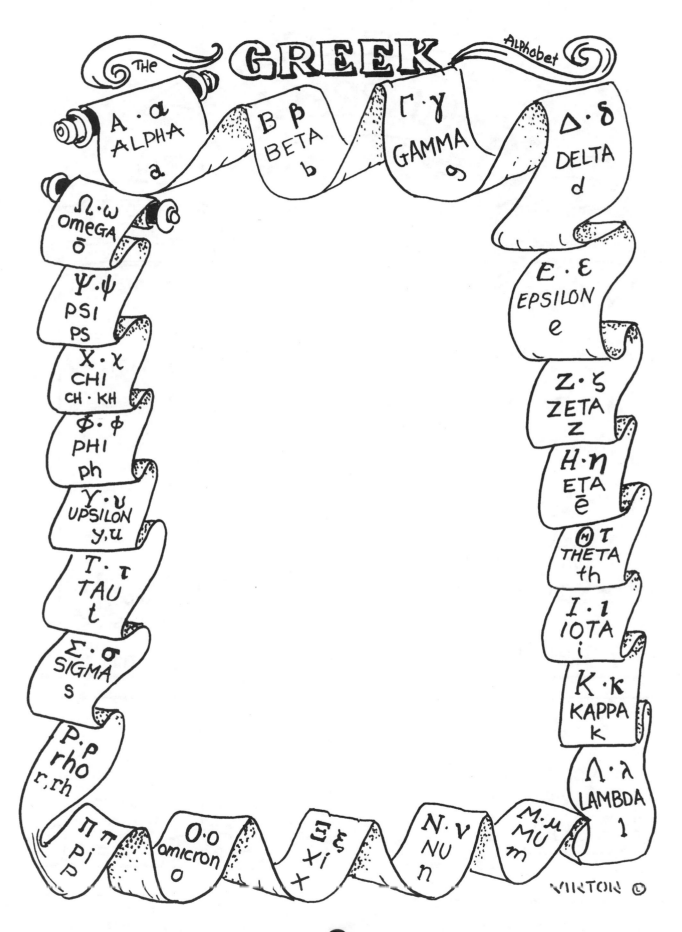

HEBREW

א	'aleph (Alef)	'
ב	beth	b
ג	gimel	g
ד	daleth	d
ה	he (heh)	h
ו	waw (vav)	w
ז	zayin	z
ח	heth (khet)	h
ט	teth (tet)	t
י	yodh (yod)	y, j
כ	kaph (kaf)	k

ל	lamedh	l
מ	mem	m
נ	nun	n
ס	samekh	s
ע	'ayin	'
פ	pe (peh)	p, f
צ	saddhe (tzadi)	s
ק	qoph (koof)	q
ר	resh	r
ש	shin	sh
ש	śin	s
ת	taw (tav)	t *

* other transliterations can be found.

VINTON ©

VINTON ©

VINTON ©

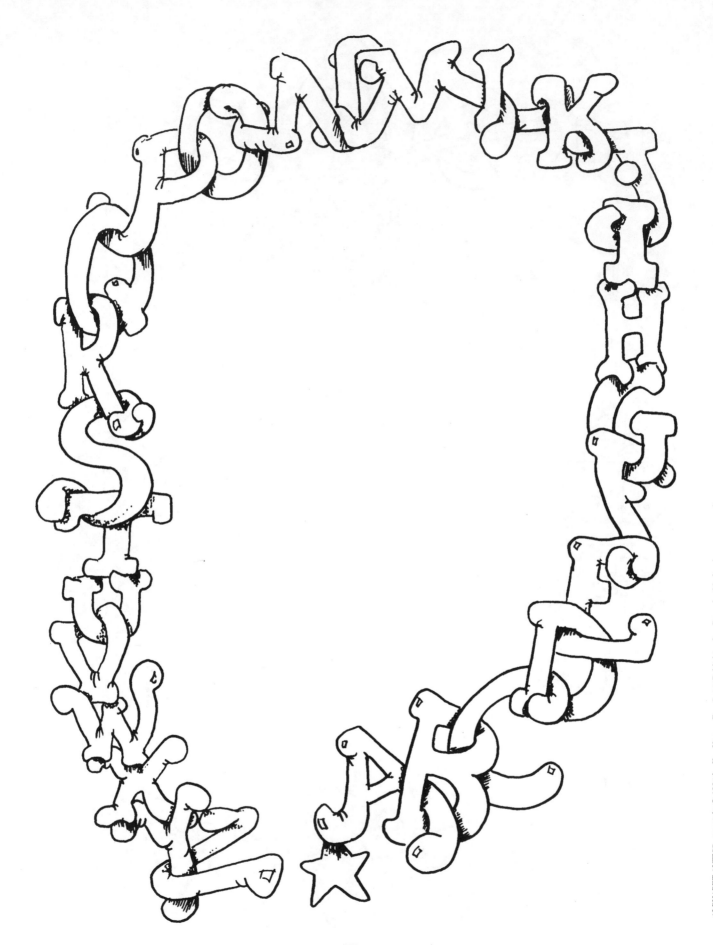

ALPHABET ANTICS, copyright © 1996 by Ken Vinton. Free Spirit Publishing Inc. Reproducible for classroom use only.

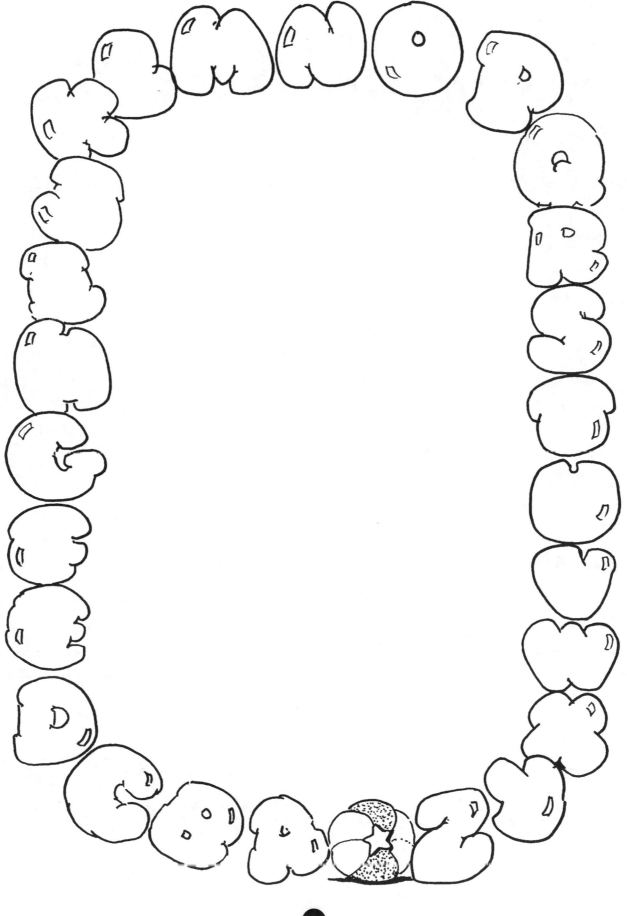

ABOUT THE AUTHOR

Ken Vinton was born on the same date the *Titanic* sank and Abraham Lincoln was shot. Also, he shares his birth date with Pete Rose . . . . Given this "great start," Ken set out to be a little different and to walk the path less traveled. He has been a contractor, an antiques dealer, a racquetball pro, and always an artist. He has been an art teacher for over 20 years, with a B.A. in Art Education from Indiana University of Pennsylvania and an M.A. in printmaking with a minor in drawing. He currently teaches art to 7th–9th graders, and he is also the author of *Write from the Edge*, published by Free Spirit in 1996. He lives a "blessed life" with his family—wife Mary Ann (a third grade teacher), children Ali and Ryan, and two cocker spaniels, Inxs and Majic—in an idyllic town in Pennsylvania.

Ken Vinton is active in the education and advancement of gifted children, and he enjoys sharing his ideas on creativity in workshops, where he is a popular and experienced presenter. His topics include:

- creativity
- cartooning
- motivation
- writing with pictures
- illustration.

If you're interested in contacting Ken about working with teachers in your district, please call or write:

Ken Vinton c/o Free Spirit Publishing Inc.
400 First Avenue North, Suite 616
Minneapolis, MN 55401-1730
(612) 338-2068
E-mail: help4kids@freespirit.com

More Books from the Free Spirited Classroom

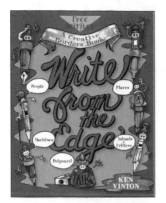

Write from the Edge
A Creative Borders Book
written and illustrated by Ken Vinton, M.A.

Fifty witty, wacky illustrated border pages promote creativity and self-expression in journal-writing, thematic lessons, writing practice, drawing, or doodling. Facing the reproducible border pages are inventive project ideas, discussion questions, and thought-provoking quotations.

$19.95; 120 pp.; s/c; illust.; 8 1/2" x 11"; Otabind lay-flat binding; 50 reproducible handout masters; Grades K–6

"The art is wonderfully creative; kids can color in the art as well as use the pages for writing. This book will be a welcome addition to your classroom, no matter what the subject!"
   —Writing Teacher magazine

Teach to Reach
Over 300 Strategies, Tips, and Helpful Hints for Teachers of All Grades
by Craig Mitchell with Pamela Espeland

A classroom teacher shares hundreds of "tricks of the trade" in this practical, encouraging collection. Teachers can turn to any page to find advice on sharpening skills, enhancing the learning environment, and making school more enjoyable for everyone.

$9.95; 200 pp.; s/c; 5 1/8" x 6"; All grades

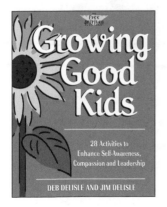

Growing Good Kids
28 Activities to Enhance Self-Awareness, Compassion, and Leadership
by Jim and Deb Delisle

These creative and fun activities build students' skills in problem solving, decision making, cooperative learning, and divergent thinking. Every activity has been teacher- and student-tested to ensure a meaningful and enjoyable learning experience.

$21.95; 160 pp.; s/c; illust.; 8 1/2" x 11"; Otabind lay-flat binding; 30 reproducible handout masters; Grades 4–8